NICK FA\

A New Light Shining

Personal
meditations
for Lent
Holy Week
and Easter

Kevin
Mayhew

First published in 2001 by
KEVIN MAYHEW LTD
Buxhall, Stowmarket, Suffolk IP14 3BW
Email: info@kevinmayhewltd.com

Scripture quotations are the author's own translation
unless otherwise stated.

9 8 7 6 5 4 3 2 1

ISBN 1 84003 842 X
Catalogue No 1500471

Cover design by Angela Selfe
Typesetting by Richard Weaver

Printed and bound in Great Britain

Contents

Introduction

A new light shining – what does that mean? We see the answer in John's Gospel where, in the opening verses, he speaks of the coming of Christ. 'In him was life, and that life was the light of all. The light shines in the darkness, and the darkness did not overcome it' (John 1:4-5). If a new day had dawned with the birth of Jesus, the light he brought was to shine ever brighter as his ministry unfolded, not even the apparent darkness of the cross finally able to obscure it.

'I am the light of the world,' said Jesus. 'Whoever follows me will never walk in darkness but will have the light of life' (John 8:12), and throughout his ministry he demonstrated the truth of that promise. In his wrestling with temptation in the wilderness and in his suffering and death he battled with the forces of darkness and emerged victorious. In his healing of the sick and seeking of the lost he brought a ray of hope to lives starved of sunshine. Through his teaching and preaching he illuminated the past and brought a sparkling vision of the future. Through his resurrection and ascension, and the events that followed, he brought a new dawn into the hearts of all who followed him.

This collection of readings, meditations and prayers, drawn and adapted from a number of my earlier books, explores some of the key moments in Jesus' life and ministry. Intended as a tool for personal devotion, it explores what he meant to those whose lives he touched, and what he means for us today. We look at the challenges he faced and the challenge he brought, beginning with his temptation and moving on to the cross and the empty tomb. Finally, we move beyond, to consider his ascension, the gift of his Spirit, and the nature of his relationship with God. The aim, throughout, is to stimulate reflection; to help you, the reader, enter into the events in such a way that they come alive for you. What must it have felt like to be one of those listening to the Sermon on the Mount; one of the Apostles gathered in the upper room; one of the crowd standing at the foot of the cross, or one of those meeting with the risen Christ? What would you have made of it all? How would you have reacted? Most important of all, how would it have changed your life?

For some of those who encountered Jesus, the experience was to change their lives. For others, we do not know quite what the outcome was. What we do know is that generations across the years have found in him the 'great light' prophesied by Isaiah; the 'day-spring from on high' foretold in Luke; the 'light shining in the darkness' proclaimed by John; the 'light of life' promised by Jesus himself. My hope, in putting together this collection of meditations, is that they may remind us of the new light God is able to shed in our hearts, today and every day.

Nick Fawcett

1
I thought I had him
The Devil

The experience of Jesus out in the wilderness was to be definitive in shaping the direction of his life and ministry, the choices he took there leading inexorably to the cross. What, though, did that experience actually entail? Did a little man with a forked tail sidle up behind his back and attempt to lead him astray? Of course not! What took place was something far more insidious yet infinitely more down to earth, for what Jesus wrestled with was ordinary pressures and desires common to us all. First, there was the temptation to meet his personal needs. After days of fasting, devoted to prayer and reflection, he was understandably hungry, so why not put his powers to good use and create some bread? Would that be to abuse his relationship with God? Not necessarily – after all, wasn't he later to feed the multitude with five loaves and two fishes? Yet Jesus knew he had to choose in the long term between serving himself or others. The impulse to turn stones into bread symbolised that dilemma. Then came the temptation to follow the way of the world. That's what it means to bow before Satan: to unquestioningly accept this world's standards and values, going along with the crowd, compromising one's convictions rather than be thought different. Jesus knew that many would happily welcome him as king, but it would be as a political Messiah, establishing an earthly kingdom. He came instead to offer us deliverance from everything that holds our spirit captive, so that we might discover the secret of the Kingdom of God. Finally, there was the temptation to put God to the test: in other words, to expect him to bow to our will rather than us bow to his. Considering what God was ultimately to ask of Jesus, a little reassurance may have seemed in order, but the point was this: he would need finally to have faith despite appearances, through death itself, with no angels there to protect him. That, and that alone, was the way to bring life to all. Don't make the mistake of seeing the temptation of Jesus as some rarefied experience divorced from our lives today. It was the opposite. The guise may be different, but anyone who is serious about Christian discipleship will face similar temptation and choices: to serve self, to go along with the world and to expect God to go along with us. The question is, will our response also be like that of Jesus?

Reading: Luke 4:1-13

Filled by the Holy Spirit, Jesus returned from the Jordan and the Spirit led him out into the wilderness, where the devil tempted him for forty days. Throughout that time he ate nothing, such that afterwards he was ravenous. The devil said to him, 'If you are the Son of God, instruct this stone to become a loaf of bread.' Jesus replied, 'It is written, "One cannot live only on bread."' Leading him up into the hills, the devil gave him a momentary glimpse of the kingdoms of this world and said to him, 'I can give all this glory and authority to you; for it has been surrendered to me and to whoever I might wish to give it. You have only to honour me for it all to be yours.' Jesus retorted, 'It is written, "Honour the Lord your God, and serve him only."' Then the devil led him to Jerusalem, setting him on the pinnacle of the temple. 'If you are the Son of God,' he said, 'hurl yourself down from here for it is written, "He will order his angels to protect you," and "They will carry you on their hands, so that you will not strike your foot against a stone."' Jesus answered him, 'It is also said, "Do not test the Lord your God too far."' Having put every temptation to him, the devil departed until a more opportune time.

Meditation

I thought I had him.
Not just once but three times I thought I'd caught him out,
    stopped him in his tracks before he'd barely had time to get
        started!

8

Prayer

Lord Jesus Christ,
    I praise you for the awesomeness of your love,
    your willingness to face death itself to bring us life.
I praise you that despite the jeers and ridicule you endured,
    your concern was always for others rather than yourself;
    that though you could have secured earthly glory,
    you chose instead the way of humility, service and self-sacrifice;
    the lonely path of the cross.
Above all, I praise you for your faithfulness to the last –
    though you could so easily have stepped down from the cross,
    you didn't;
    though you could have saved yourself,
    you preferred instead to save the world.
However often I hear it,
    still I am amazed by the magnitude of your love
    and the awesomeness of your sacrifice.
Receive my praise and accept my worship,
    for your name's sake.
Amen.

11
He was silent
Mary, wife of Clopas

'Were you there when they crucified my Lord?' So asks that lovely and powerful hymn so often sung on or around Good Friday. The answer of course is that we weren't. Yet, how must it have felt for those who were – those like Mary, the wife of Clopas, who stood and watched to the bitter end? Their suffering must have rivalled that of Jesus, as they saw the one they loved endure such pain and anguish. What did they make of it all? Did they see only despair and defeat? Was there nothing to hold on to, no chink of light in the darkness? Or did they, like the centurion at the foot of the cross, see something in the way Jesus died that spoke, even then, of God being present; of God being at work in a way that, though they could not understand it, pointed to an eternal purpose beyond death itself?

Reading: John 19:25, 28-30

Close to the cross of Jesus there stood his mother, his mother's sister Mary, the wife of Clopas, and Mary Magdalene . . . Realising that everything was accomplished, Jesus called out (fulfilling the Scripture), 'I am thirsty!' A jar full of wine-vinegar had been set there, so they soaked a sponge in it, impaled it on a branch of hyssop, and held it up to his mouth. Having drunk the 'wine', Jesus said, 'It is finished!' Then, bowing his head, he gave up his spirit.

Meditation

He was silent,
   quite still,
   his body limp and lifeless,
   like a rag doll,
   like a broken puppet,
   and I thanked God that at last it was over,
   his ordeal finally ended.
Only it wasn't –
   not quite.
He moved again –
   just the faintest twitch,
   the last flickering ember of life –
   but enough to prolong our hopes,
   enough to prolong his pain.
He was still breathing,
   still suffering.
We watched wretchedly, torn by conflicting desires –
   the longing to see him come down and prove his enemies
      wrong;
   the longing to see him find peace in the cold embrace of death.
But suddenly his eyes were open,
   wide,
   bright,
   triumphant;
   lips were moving,
   eager,
   excited,
   exultant;
   and his voice rang out:
   'It is finished!'
An acknowledgement of defeat, some said afterwards,
   a last despairing cry of sorrow.
But it wasn't,
   not for those who heard it,
   not for those with ears to hear.

It was altogether different –
    like sunshine after storm,
    like rain after drought,
    like laughter after tears –
    gloriously unexpected,
    wonderfully surprising.
He had stooped and conquered,
    staked all and won.
Defeat was victory,
    darkness was light,
    death was life.
I didn't see it then, mind you,
    I can't pretend that.
It was just a glimpse at the time,
    a glimmer barely understood.
But what I did see, with sudden staggering clarity,
    was that until that moment,
    until that last victorious shout,
    he had lived with the awful burden of holding the world's fate
        in his hands
    and wondering whether he could see it through.
At last it was done –
    he had honoured his calling,
    fulfilled his mission,
    walked the way of the cross.
It was finished,
    and with a song in his heart and light in his eyes
    he bowed his head and surrendered his spirit.

Prayer

Lord Jesus Christ,
    living in the light of Easter, I can forget sometimes the
        darkness of Good Friday,
    but I remember today that for those who saw you suffering on
        the cross
    there could be no mistaking the truth,
    no escaping the awfulness of the moment.
You endured the pain of betrayal,
    the hurt of denial,
    the humiliation of mockery and, finally,
    the awful isolation of separation from your Father
    as you took humankind's sins on your shoulders –
    and you did it for such as me!
Lord Jesus,
    I marvel at your love;
    at the fact that you were willing to go not just part of the way
    but the whole way to redeem the world.
I marvel that you were willing to experience death
    so that I might taste life.
Teach me today to appreciate the wonder of your sacrifice
    and to recognise all that it means in so many ways.
Amen.

12

I just can't understand what happened
One of the guards at the tomb

You can't keep a good man down, so they say, and in the case of Jesus that was seen to be true in a way that was to astonish friend and foe alike. His enemies had resolved to destroy him, and as they cut him down from the cross and sealed him in a tomb, they must have believed they had finally succeeded. Even so, they left nothing to chance, placing a guard outside the tomb just to make sure no one could steal his body away. Whichever way you looked at things, it looked like the end – there could surely be no way back. Yet the next day, to their surprise, the stone was rolled away and the tomb empty; their worst fears realised. How could it be? What could have happened? They had done everything in their power, and it had not been enough. In a world where hatred and evil continue to exert their hold, we need reminding of that truth as much as ever. We need to remember that however hopeless things may seem, and however strong the forces we are up against, the love of God is stronger. Though much may fight against him and though evil may sometimes seem victorious, ours is a God who will finally triumph and who assures us of ultimate victory in turn.

Reading: Matthew 28:11-15a

Some of the guards went into the city and told the chief priests what had happened. After the priests had called together the elders, they formulated a plan to give a generous bribe to the soldiers, telling them, 'You must say this: "His followers came during the night and made off with him while we were sleeping." If the governor gets to hear of this, we will reassure him and keep you out of trouble.' So the guards took the money and did as instructed.

Meditation

I just can't understand what happened,
>   how that body could have disappeared like that from under
>   our very noses.
Oh, I know what some have suggested –
>   that his disciples stole him away while we were asleep,
>   that we took bribes to look the other way,
>   even that we nipped off for a spot of refreshment,
>   but take it from me, it's nonsense,
>   for we were there the whole time,
>   watching like a hawk,
>   on the lookout for any suspicious goings on,
>   and I can tell you that no one came near the place all night,
>   not until those women arrived early the next morning,
>   and discovered that the tomb was empty.
You think *they* were shocked?
How about *us*!
We just stood there, gaping in amazement,
>   unable to believe our eyes.
It couldn't be,
>   that's what we kept saying,
>   no way –
>   but it was,
>   no doubt about it.
We should have come clean, there and then,
>   told the world what we knew, even though it made no sense;
>   but it wasn't that easy,
>   for we knew that our jobs,
>   even perhaps our lives, were on the line –
>   the penalty for failure.
So when those priests sidled up with their offer of money –
>   a generous bonus to keep our mouths shut
>   and the promise to square things with the governor –
>   well, understandably we took it;
>   we'd have been fools not to.

Yet it still rankled,
    still stuck in the craw –
    not just the dressing-down we received, fierce though that was,
    but the stain on our reputation,
    the stigma of supposedly having fallen down on the job,
    so I'm taking the chance, at last, to put the record straight.
There was no foul-up that night –
    we knew our job and we stuck to it faithfully.
Don't forget we were Roman soldiers,
    proud of our legion,
    dedicated to our job –
    we'd a reputation to keep up,
    and there was no way we were going to let the side down.
No, don't look at us, we weren't to blame.
But if not us, then who?
And, more important, how?
One thing's for certain,
    that body was there when they sealed the tomb –
    we saw it for ourselves –
    but next morning it was gone,
    vanished apparently into thin air!
Something happened that night;
    something quite extraordinary.
Can you explain it?
I wish I could.

Prayer

Lord Jesus Christ,
> I do not understand how the stone was rolled away from the
> > tomb;
> how you appeared to Mary in the garden
> and to disciples on the Emmaus Road;
> how you walked through locked doors to be with your disciples
> appearing from nowhere to stand among them.

What I do understand is this:
> that you changed the lives of all who met you,
> turning sorrow into celebration,
> despair into hope
> and doubt into faith;
> and that you continue to meet with people today,
> reshaping lives through your life-giving Spirit,
> granting joy, peace and a sense of purpose
> such as I would never have imagined possible.

I do not understand,
> but I believe,
> I rejoice
> and I greet you as my Lord and Saviour
> in grateful worship.

Amen.

13
He was back!
Peter

It wasn't just the enemies of Jesus who imagined his life was over when his body was sealed in the tomb; it was his friends too. They had stood by the cross and seen him writhe in agony; they had watched with their own eyes as he drew his last breath; and they had seen the spear thrust deep into his side, final proof that he was indisputably dead. We can scarcely imagine how desperate that moment must have been for them, and how bleak the ensuing day must have seemed. It wasn't just their Master who had been destroyed but their world as well, for everything they had hoped for, believed in and lived by was suddenly snuffed out. How could they make sense of it? How could God have let it happen? How could they face the future? Yet suddenly joy was born again and hope resurrected, as Jesus stood before them, alive and well. They were not alone after all! God had not deserted them! Their faith was not in vain! We too may sometimes feel that life is empty and hopeless. Confronted by the death of a loved one or the realisation of our own mortality, overwhelmed by trouble, crushed by disappointment or weighed down by doubts, we may find ourselves facing the dark night of the soul where all seems devoid of meaning. Easter reminds us that not only did Jesus come back from the grave as he had promised, but that he also brought new life to his followers – new beginnings, new purpose, new hope – a resurrection now that anticipates the resurrection still to come.

Reading: Luke 24:36-43

Even as they spoke, Jesus stood among them in person, saying, 'Peace be with you.' However, they were shaken and terrified, convinced he was a ghost. He said to them, 'Why are you troubled, and why are your hearts so full of questions? Look at my hands and feet; is it not me? Touch me and see; a ghost does not have flesh and bones such as you see I have.' Having said this, he showed them his hands and his feet, but they still could scarcely believe it, so overcome were they with joy and wonder. Then he said to them, 'Have you any food?' They gave him a piece of broiled fish, which he took and ate in their presence.

Meditation

He was back!
Back in the land of the living, just when we'd given up hope!
Three days it had been,
    three days of dark despair as slowly the truth sank home –
    our Lord, laid in a tomb,
    dead and buried,
    never to walk this earth again.
We couldn't believe it at first,
    none of us,
    even though we'd seen it for ourselves.
We expected to wake up any moment to find it was all a dream,
    a dreadful mistake that had somehow taken us in.
But as the numbness passed so the reality hit us,
    and the pain began in earnest.
It was an end to everything –
    our plans,
    our hopes,
    our dreams.
There was nothing left to live for,
    that's how we felt –
    we'd pinned our hopes on him,
    and he was gone.
Only he wasn't!
He was there, meeting Mary in the garden as she broke her heart
    beside the tomb.

He was there, on the Emmaus Road, as two followers trudged
    slowly home, their world in tatters.
He was there, speaking to Thomas, breaking through his
    disbelief!
He was there, standing among us in the upper room!
He was back in the land of the living,
    and suddenly so were we –
    faith rekindled,
    hope renewed,
    joy reborn,
    life beginning again!

Prayer

Lord Jesus Christ,
    just when it looked all over,
    when the world had written you off
    and even your disciples given you up,
    you came back –
    defeat revealed as victory.
Teach me what that means for me today –
    to recognise that it brings not only the promise of eternal life,
    but good news for life here and now.
Help me to understand that whatever tragedies I may suffer,
    whatever obstacles I may face,
    whatever disappointments I may experience,
    I can bounce back from them with your help,
    for you are a God able to transform even the darkest moments
    and lead me through them into the light of your love.
Gladly, then, I put my hand in yours,
    knowing that in life or death you will never fail or forsake me.
To you be praise and glory,
    now and always.
Amen.

14
We stood there, speechless for a moment
James

They had seen death, they had seen resurrection, and for the disciples the sight of the risen Christ back among them must have seemed the most wonderful thing they could ever hope to see. No wonder they asked the question that had been on their lips since his return: 'Lord, is this the time when you will restore the kingdom to Israel?' It had to be, surely! What more could be revealed than had been revealed to them already? The answer was not long coming, as suddenly Jesus was taken from them and they were left wide-eyed with wonder and amazement. Whatever the precise event behind the language, one thing is clear – their picture of Christ had been far too small, their understanding of his purpose much too narrow. For he came not just to restore Israel but to redeem the world, not to rule on earth but to be enthroned in heaven. They had glimpsed the man but not the face of God beneath. They believed they saw the whole picture, when they saw but one piece of the jigsaw. Suddenly they had to think again, for Jesus was greater than they had begun to imagine. The same, I suspect, may be true for us all.

Reading: Acts 1:6-11
Coming together, they asked him, 'Lord, is this the time when you will restore the kingdom of Israel?' He replied, 'It is not for you to know the time or seasons that the Father has laid down by his own authority, but you will receive power when the Holy Spirit comes upon you and you will be my witnesses both in Jerusalem, and all Judea and Samaria, and to the ends of the earth.' Having said this,

and while they were watching, he was lifted up, and a cloud obscured him from their sight. While he was going and they were staring up into the sky, suddenly two men clothed in white stood next to them. They said, 'Men of Galilee, why do you stand staring up into the sky? This Jesus, who has been taken from you up into heaven, will come back in the same way that you saw him go.'

Meditation

We stood there, speechless for a moment,
    struck dumb by the enormity of it all,
    for he was gone,
    plucked away from before our very eyes,
    and, quite simply, we were lost for words,
    stunned into silence.
It wasn't the first time, you see,
    we'd lost him once already –
    watched in horror as he was nailed to a cross, sealed in a tomb –
    and we'd been devastated,
    convinced we could never bounce back from such a blow.
We wouldn't have, either,
    not by ourselves;
    but suddenly he was back –
    there in the garden,
    there by the roadside,
    there in the upper room –
    our Lord, alive, risen, victorious,
    death unable to hold him!
I just can't tell you how wonderful that was,
    how our hearts skipped and our spirits soared each time we
        saw him.
We felt certain nothing could ever again destroy our happiness,
    for he had taken on the last enemy and emerged triumphant!
Life, all at once, pulsated with promise,
    no problem too great for us,

no challenge too daunting,
for with Christ by our side what had we to fear?
Yet suddenly, as we stood there that day gazing into heaven,
    he was by our side no longer,
    and for an awful moment it seemed as though all our hopes
        had disappeared again,
    vanishing with him like a bubble on the wind.
Only, of course, this time it was different,
    for we'd made time to listen,
    paid heed to his warnings,
    and we understood that, as he had departed, so finally he
    would return.
You should see us now,
    our faith, if anything, stronger today than it's ever been!
We've spoken more boldly
    and witnessed more powerfully than I thought possible –
    preaching the word,
    healing the sick,
    renewing the weak,
    uplifting the broken-hearted,
    carrying the good news of Jesus far and wide.
And I'll tell you why:
    his going that day has somehow brought him closer
        than he's ever been before,
    filling our whole being – body, mind and soul –
    transforming our every thought and word and deed.
He's here,
    he's there,
    he's everywhere;
    no person beyond his love,
    no situation beyond his purpose,
    for he has not simply risen,
    he has ascended –
    Jesus, the man who lived and died amongst us,
    who shared our flesh and blood,
    one with the Father,

Lord of lords and King of kings,
nothing in heaven or earth able to separate us
from the wonder of his love.
And when I think of all that means,
once more I'm struck dumb sometimes,
stunned into silence by the enormity of it all,
for it's wonderful, isn't it? –
almost too wonderful for words!

Prayer

Lord Jesus Christ,
you were brought low,
yet you have been lifted high.
You were the servant of all,
yet you are above all and beyond all.
You were despised and rejected,
yet your name is exalted above all names.
You were fully human,
yet you are divine.
You were taken into heaven,
yet you are here now by my side.
You are higher than my highest thoughts,
greater than my mind can ever grasp,
and so, with all your people in every age,
I confess you as my risen Saviour,
the King of kings and Lord of lords,
to the glory of God the Father.
Amen.

15

We shouldn't have been surprised
Peter

'I just can't do it!' How often have we claimed that, or something similar? If so, think again, for today we remember how twelve disciples, who must have said and thought much the same, were transformed in the space of a few moments into those for whom nothing apparently was beyond them. What was their secret? There wasn't one, for the change within them had nothing to do with their efforts but everything to do with God's. It took simply the breath of his Spirit to bring about one of the most astonishing transformations in history, and to set into motion the extraordinary events of what we sometimes call 'the day of Pentecost'. Yet Pentecost is not about *one* day but *every* day, for the gift of the Spirit is a continuous experience intended for all. You and I, like those who have gone before us, are called to be Pentecost people, living and working in ways we might once have thought beyond us to the glory of Christ. Have we risen to the challenge?

Reading: Acts 2:1-12

When the day of Pentecost dawned, they were gathered in one place. Suddenly, a sound like the rush of a mighty wind came from heaven, filling the house where they were sitting. After that, tongues of fire appeared that divided so that a tongue rested on each of them. They were all filled with the Holy Spirit, and began to speak in various tongues, as the Spirit enabled them. It so happened that there were devout Jews from every nation under heaven residing in Jerusalem at this time, and hearing this sound the crowd gathered in bewilderment, since each heard them speaking their native language. Astounded and incredulous, they asked, 'Are not all these who are speaking Galileans? How is it, then, that we each hear our own native language? Parthians, Medes and Elamites; residents of Mesopotamia, Judea, Cappadocia, Pontus, Asia, Phrygia, Pamphylia, Egypt and the parts of Libya belonging to Cyrene; visitors from Rome, both Jews and proselytes; and Cretans and Arabs – we hear them speaking about God's deeds of power in our own tongue.' All were bemused and baffled, saying to one another, 'What can this mean?'

Meditation

We shouldn't have been surprised,
    not if we'd had any sense;
    it was what we'd been told to expect,
    what he'd promised us,
    but we never imagined anything quite so extraordinary.
We were waiting, it's true,
    gathered together as so often before,
    but we'd been doing that for days
    and our confidence had taken a hammering.
We were going through the motions, that's all,
    telling each other he hadn't forgotten us,
    talking of the future as though we still believed in it,
    yet wondering in our hearts if there was anything to look
        forward to.
I mean, when all was said and done,
    what could we hope to achieve?
What reason to think that we,
    a motley bunch if ever there was one,
    should fare better than our master?
We wanted to carry on his work, don't get me wrong.

We wanted to tell people what had happened,
    help them find faith for themselves,
    but how could we even hope to begin?
So we kept the doors locked,
    sung our hymns,
    said our prayers,
    and hid our doubts.
Until, suddenly, it happened!
I can't properly describe it even now,
    but it changed our lives.
It was as though a mighty wind blew away the cobwebs,
    a refreshing breeze revived our flagging faith,
    a breath of air stirred our spirits;
    as though a tiny spark rekindled our confidence,
    a tongue of fire set our hearts aflame,
    a raging inferno swept our fears away;
    as though life had begun again,
    the world become a different place,
    and each of us been born anew.
I know that doesn't make sense,
    but it's the best I can do.
You'll have to experience it for yourself to understand.
    and you can, just as we did.
Believe me, we never would have thought it possible,
    despite all Jesus said to us.
We were lost,
    lonely,
    frightened,
    hopelessly aware of our weaknesses,
    searching for any strengths.
We never thought we'd change a soul,
    let alone the world,
    but that's because we had no idea how God could change us!

Prayer

Gracious God,
    I thank you for those special life-changing moments that
    give joy and fulfilment such as I never imagined possible.
I thank you especially for the great gift of your Holy Spirit –
    an experience that transformed the life of the Apostles,
    changed the lives of countless believers across the
        centuries,
    and is able to reshape lives here and now.
Open my heart, mind and soul to your living presence
    so that I may know your life-changing power within me.
Deepen my faith,
    enrich my experience,
    strengthen my commitment
    enlarge my vision,
    and so may I know you better
    and be equipped to serve you more fully,
    to the glory of your name.
Amen.

16
I didn't know what he was on about
John

Trinity Sunday probably captures the imagination less than any other day in the Christian year. To a point, this is understandable, for it is concerned with abstract doctrine rather than historical events; a doctrine, moreover, that has perplexed theologians and ordinary believers alike across the centuries. Yet, complex though the issues may be, we do well to reflect on them, for, if anything, this day should capture the imagination more than any other, reminding us of the breathtaking reality that we describe as God. We try to pin that reality down as best we can; to talk about our experience in terms of God the Father, the Son and the Holy Spirit; but we are always at best simply grasping at the truth, God's ways not our ways nor his thoughts our thoughts. Thank God for this day that reminds us of that simple inescapable fact. Make use of it to deepen your faith and enrich your experience of his living, loving, and transforming presence.

Reading: John 15:12-16, 26-27

My commandment is this: that you love one another as I have loved you. There is no greater love than laying down one's life for one's friends. I count you my friends if you do what I command you. No longer do I call you servants, because a servant has no knowledge of the master's intentions. Instead, I have called you friends, because I have communicated everything to you that I have heard from my Father. You did not choose me but I chose you, and appointed you to go and bear fruit; enduring fruit, so that whatever you ask for in my name from the Father he will give you. When the Advocate comes – the Spirit of truth emanating

from the Father whom I will send to you from the Father – he will
bear witness concerning me. You also are to witness to me, because
you have been with me from the start.

Meditation

I didn't know what he was on about at the time,
    not the faintest idea,
    despite the way I nodded
    and attempted to smile in the right places.
The Advocate?
The Son who comes from the Father?
What did it all mean?
We believed he was sent by God, yes –
    called to reveal his will,
    build his kingdom –
    but was he saying more,
    pointing to a closer relationship?
It seemed so,
    yet; try as we might, we just couldn't get our heads round it.
'The Lord our God is one', isn't that what we'd always been told?
Indeed, he said it himself,
    made no bones about it,
    so how could he also tell us,
    'He who has seen me has seen the Father'?
We were baffled, there's no other word for it,
    and when he went on to talk about the Spirit of truth,
    the one his Father would send in his name,
    quite simply, by then, we were reeling,
    unable to make head or tail of what he was getting at.
'Do we understand now, though?' you ask.
Well no, we don't actually,
    funnily enough, if we try to explain it
    we still struggle as much as ever,
    the more we try the worse the knots we tie ourselves in.

Yet, strange though it may sound, it makes sense despite that –
for day after day, year after year, we've tasted the truth,
the reality of Father, Son and Holy Spirit.
We look up,
to the stars and the sky,
the wonder of the heavens,
and God is there, enthroned in splendour,
sovereign over all.
We look around,
at the world he's given,
its awesome beauty,
its endless interest,
its bountiful provision,
and he is there,
stretching out his hand in love,
inviting us to share in its wonder.
We look nearby,
at family and friends,
beyond, to the nameless faces of the multitude,
and he is there,
giving and receiving,
waiting to feed and to be fed.
We look within,
at our aching souls,
our pleading hearts,
and he is there,
breathing new life,
new purpose within us.
One God, yes,
but a God we meet in different guises,
different ways,
three in one and one in three.
It sounds odd, I know,
and take it from me, you'll never explain it, no matter how you try,
yet don't worry, for what finally matters is this:
though words may fail you, the experience never will!

Prayer

Mighty God,
    beyond all space and time,
    greater than my mind can grasp,
    ruler over all that is, has been and shall be –
    I worship you.
Loving Father,
    kind and merciful,
    full of goodness and compassion,
    constantly watching over me and directing my steps –
    I praise you.
Saviour Christ,
    flesh of my flesh yet the living image of God,
    sharing my humanity yet one with the Father,
    loving to the point of death yet bringer of life,
    I acknowledge you.
Holy Spirit,
    free and mysterious,
    source of guidance and inspiration,
    filling my heart and mind,
    I welcome you.
Mighty God,
    Father, Son and Holy Spirit,
    I greet you with awe, joy and thanksgiving,
    celebrating all you mean to me
    and everything you have done in my life.
To you be glory and honour,
    this and every day.
Amen.

And I was close,
    even *he*, I expect, would give me that.
Oh, he started off well enough –
    sure of his destiny,
    confident of his ability to grasp it.
But then he would have, wouldn't he,
    coming out into the wilderness like that
    straight after his baptism,
    heart still skipping within him,
    the memory fresh,
    the voice of God continuing to ring in his ears.
But forty days on –
    forty days of gnawing hunger, desert heat and night-time chill –
    and then it was a different story,
    hard then to think of anything
    but the pain in his belly and the simple comforts of home.
So I saw my chance
    and made my move.
Nothing crude or clumsy –
    no point scaring him off unnecessarily –
    just a subtle whisper,
    a sly suggestion,
    'Turn this stone into bread.'
And he was tempted, don't be fooled.
I could see by the gleam in his eyes, and the way he licked his lips,
    that, if you'll pardon the expression, he was chewing it over.
It wouldn't have taken much to make him crack, I'm certain of it;
    one whiff of a fresh-baked loaf and I'm sure he'd have given in –
    why didn't I think of it!
Only then he remembered those cursed Scriptures of his,
    and all my hard work was undone in a moment:
    'One cannot live only on bread.'
It was a setback,
    but I pressed on, confident I was making ground.
And soon after he was up on the mountains,
    the world stretching out before him as far as the eye could see.

'All this is yours!' I whispered. 'Just forget this Messiah business
    and grab it while you can.'
Oh, you may sneer with hindsight at my methods,
    but it's worked before, I can tell you –
    many a lofty ideal sacrificed on the altar of ambition.
But not Jesus –
    in fact this time not even a suggestion of compromise:
'It is written, "Honour the Lord your God, and serve him only."'
So I took him in his imagination up on to the temple
    and played my trump card:
    'Go on,' I urged him, 'Throw yourself off.
    'If you are who you think you are, God will save you,
    for *it is written:*
    "He will order his angels to protect you.
    They will carry you on their hands so that you will not strike
    your foot against a stone."'
A master-stroke, so I thought,
    quoting his own Scriptures at him like that,
    and let's face it, we all like a little reassurance,
        however strong our faith;
    the knowledge, should the worst come to the worst, that
        there'll be someone to bail us when we need it.
'Why should he be any different?' I reasoned –
    he was as human as the next man,
    as vulnerable as the rest of your miserable kind.
But somehow, even then he held firm:
    'It is said,' he answered, "Do not test the Lord your God too
        far."'
Well that was it,
    I knew I was beaten.
There was nothing left to throw at him,
    so I slithered away to lick my wounds.
But I'll be back, you mark my words,
    and next time, when it's his whole life in the balance,
    a question of do or die,
    then we'll see what he's really made of, won't we?
Then we'll see which of us is finally the stronger.

Prayer

Lord of all,
> you remind me that even Jesus faced temptation during his
>> lifetime –
> the temptation to compromise his convictions,
> to abandon his calling,
> to serve himself rather than others.

Teach me to recognise the many similar temptations *I* face in turn,
> some easy to spot but others so subtle and insidious
> that I give in to them without even realising it.

Give me a clear sense of what you would have me do
> and all you would have me be,
> and grant me the courage and commitment I need
> to stand firm whenever temptation strikes.

So may I stay true to you,
> and offer you my faithful service,
> in the name of Christ.

Amen.

2
Can you believe what he told us?
Listener to the Sermon on the Mount

Love your enemies – few words better sum up the distinctive message of Jesus that turns the accepted values of this world on their head. We applaud such ideals, but can we truly live by them? So long as we're talking in abstract terms, the answer is probably yes – after all, few of us have enemies in any meaningful sense of the word. We may find some people hard to get on with, but few wish us harm. How would we feel, though, if we had lost a loved one in a Northern Ireland bomb blast or the terrorist attack on the World Trade Centre? Viewed in that light, suddenly the nature of the challenge becomes clearer. Could you love those responsible? I'm not sure I could. Could you feel anything other than bitterness, hatred and a desire for revenge? I know I'd struggle. More to the point, what does loving your enemies mean in practice, and is it a realistic option in our modern world? Can we afford to let hatred and violence pass unchallenged, inviting more of the same? Could the US government and its allies, for example, have 'turned the other cheek' following the Trade Centre carnage? Such questions do not admit to easy answers, and Christians should beware of offering them. Ethical issues are rarely black and white. Yet, at the same time, meeting one evil with another – an eye for an eye and a tooth for a tooth – is clearly not a viable alternative, serving merely to perpetuate the cycle of mistrust and intolerance and leading to yet more suffering and bloodshed. The way of Christ speaks of a willingness to forgive, of wishing good rather than evil, and of meeting rejection with acceptance and hatred with love. It is not an easy way, by any reckoning, yet ultimately the bleak lessons of history testify that it is the only way.

Reading: Matthew 5:38-45

You have heard it said, 'An eye for an eye and a tooth for a tooth'. But I tell you, 'Do not resist an evildoer. On the contrary, if someone slaps you on the cheek, offer the other in turn; if anyone sues you for your coat, give your cloak as well; and if anyone compels you to go one mile, go two miles instead. Give to whoever begs from you, and do not turn your back on anyone who needs to borrow from you.' You have heard it said, 'You shall love your neighbour and hate your enemy.' But I tell you, 'Love your enemies and pray for those who cruelly use you, so that you may become children of your heavenly Father; for he causes his sun to rise on the evil and the good, and the rain to fall on the just and unjust.'

Meditation

Can you believe what he told us?
Love your enemies, that's what he said!
Pray for those who abuse you,
    and if someone slaps you in the face, turn the other cheek!
Well, I ask you, what sort of talk is that?
He's on another planet, this fellow –
    cloud-cuckoo land!
Oh it sounds wonderful, granted,
    but can you see it working?
I can't.
No, we have to be sensible about these things,
    realistic.
We'd all like the world to be different,
    but it's no use pretending, is it?
Love your enemies –
    where will that get us?
They'll see us coming a mile off!
And as for turning the other cheek –
    well, *you* can if you want to, but not me;

I'll give them one back with interest –
  either that or run for it!
I'll tell you what though,
  we listened to him,
  all of us –
  just about the biggest crowd I've ever seen,
  hanging on to his every word,
  listening like I've rarely known people listen before.
Why?
Well you could see he meant what he was saying for one thing –
  the way he dealt with the hecklers and cynics:
  never losing his cool,
  never lashing out in frustration,
  ready to suffer for his convictions if that's what it took.
He practised what he preached, and there aren't many you can
      say that about, are there?
But it was more than that.
Like it or not, it was that incredible message of his,
  that crazy message so different from any we'd ever heard
      before –
  impractical,
  unworkable,
  yet irresistible.
It gave us a glimpse of the way life could be,
  the way it should be –
  and he actually made us feel that one day it might be!
No, I'm not convinced, sad to say –
  life's just not like that –
  but I wish it was.
I wish I had the courage to try his way,
  the faith to give it a go,
  for we've been trying the way of the world for as long as I can
      remember,
  and look where that's got us!

Prayer

Lord Jesus,
>we are told that the strongest survive,
>that we need to look after number one,
>that in this world it's a question of never mind the rest
>so long as we're all right.

Yet you speak of another way –
>the way of humility, sacrifice and self denial,
>of putting the interests of others before our own.

You stand accepted wisdom on its head,
>claiming that the meek shall inherit the earth,
>and that those who are willing to lose their lives
>will truly find them.

Lord Jesus,
>it is hard to believe in this way of yours,
>and harder still to live by it –
>it runs contrary to everything I know about human nature,
>yet I have seen all too clearly where the world's way leads –
>the hurt, sorrow and division it so often causes.

Give me faith and courage, then,
>to live out the foolishness of the gospel,
>and so to bring closer your kingdom, here on earth.

In your name I ask it.
Amen.

3

It's a great picture, isn't it!

Another listener to the Sermon on the Mount

Several years ago, I spent an unforgettable holiday in Northumberland, a county that boasts what is surely one of the most beautiful and unspoilt stretches of coastline in the country. There is so much to enjoy there: perfect sandy beaches, craggy cliffs, remote islands, seabirds, seals, and so much else. What captured my imagination most, however, were the castles in the area; in particular, Lindisfarne and Bamburgh, both perched high on rocky promontories above the sea. They have stood on their massive bulwarks for centuries, resisting the pounding of the waves and the assault of the elements, and, no doubt, they will stand for centuries to come. Contrast that with the situation further down the coast, in Norfolk and Suffolk. Here, where the cliffs are much softer, the sea is inexorably eating its way into them, to the point that a succession of houses have toppled over the edge during the last decade. The foundations of these properties had looked secure when first laid, but time has taken its toll, ruthlessly laying them bare. Reading the familiar parable of Jesus concerning the wise and foolish builders, we may believe that we have built our lives on firm foundations, but we do well to reflect on his words. Remember that Jesus didn't just say 'everyone who hears my words is like a wise person who built his house on rock' but 'everyone who hears my words *and acts upon them*'. The two are very different. It's not hearing the words of Jesus that matters, not even accepting they are true; it's whether they make a difference to who we are, whether they change the way we live, whether we hear and act upon them. Are we still so sure we've built our house on the rock?

Reading: Matthew 7:24-27

Everyone who hears my words and acts on them will be like a wise man who built his house on rock. The rain fell, the floods came, and the gales blasted and battered that house, but it did not collapse, because its foundations were on rock. On the other hand, everyone who hears my words and fails to act on them will be like a fool who built his house on sand. The rain fell, and the floods came, and the winds blasted and battered that house, and it crashed – and what a collapse it was!

Meditation

It's a great picture, isn't it!
A wonderful, almost ridiculous, contrast!
The wise man building his house on sure foundations
    and the fool building his on the sand.
Could anyone be so stupid?
You wouldn't have thought so, would you?
And I was confident of one thing:
    you wouldn't catch me making such a mistake,
    not the slightest danger of that at all.
No, I understood that there's more to life than meets the eye,
    more than money or material possessions, status or success,
    for none of those are certain when the going gets hard
        and the storms break over you.
I knew there had to be something else,
    and in Jesus I thought I'd found it.
As I listened to his teaching and marvelled at his ministry,
    as I saw for myself lives transformed,
    broken, battered individuals healed, renewed, forgiven,
    I decided that here was what life is all about,
    and I rejoiced in his message of love and forgiveness.
I drank in his every word,
    determined to make the blessings he spoke of mine,
    confident of experiencing the joys of his kingdom.

Only then it came, just as he'd warned it would do –
    the rain fell,
    the floods rose,
    the wind blew and beat against me –
    and, with a sickening crash, I fell.
That's right, you heard me,
    I fell!
Why?
Because I thought I'd obeyed, and I hadn't,
    I thought I'd been wise, and I'd been a fool,
    I thought I'd listened, and I'd barely heard,
    ignoring the one thing that really mattered.
'Everyone,' he said, 'who hears these words of mine
    and acts upon them
    will be like a wise man who built his house on rock.'
I'd done the first but not the second,
    the faith I professed all words and no actions,
    and now, when the moment came, I was found wanting,
    life crumbling into the sand after all.
I'd come close, yet not close enough,
    recognising that Jesus was the way, the truth and the life,
    but accepting it only with my head,
    not my heart.
Don't make my mistake.
Don't sit back believing you've done all that needs doing
    or, like me, you may be in for an unwelcome surprise.
It's not hearing his words that matters,
    not even accepting they are true;
    it's whether they make a difference to who you are,
    whether they change the way you live,
    whether you hear and act upon them.

To pray

Lord Jesus Christ,
    I like to think I have founded my life firmly upon you,
    but the reality is not always as I imagine.
Though I declare my faith in you and profess your name;
    though I talk of commitment and speak of service,
    there is a danger of this being all show and no substance,
    a matter of words rather than deeds.
I fail truly to listen to what you would tell me;
    I am slow to reflect on what discipleship really means
    and offer you only a part of my life,
    keeping the rest back for fear or what you might ask of me.
Like the foolish builder
    I hear your words but do not act upon them,
    my good intentions never translated into action.
Forgive me, despite your guidance,
    for building my life on sand rather than rock.
Open my ears, my mind and my heart,
    so that I may not only hear what you would say to me
    but also respond with body, mind and soul,
    to the glory of your name.
Amen.

4

I felt sorry for Martha, I really did
Mary, sister of Martha

Over the past few years, I have found myself becoming increasingly busy, as writing and editing commitments have built up. I'm not complaining – better that than having no work at all – but there has been a price to pay; namely, the loss of time to stop and stare. Does that matter? On the face of it, no, for I'm getting more done than ever before, but am I focusing on the right things, and maintaining a proper balance between work and leisure, family and other commitments? Such questions apply to every one of us, for we can all become sucked into the rat race, preoccupied with Rudyard Kipling's 'unforgiving minute'. However much we do, there will always be something else calling for our attention. We need sometimes to pause and ask ourselves what we are doing and why; to consider the deeper things of life and sort out our priorities. Above all, we need to make time to reflect on ultimate realities; or, in other words, upon God. Traditionally, Lent is such a time, reminding us of the moments Jesus spent in the wilderness contemplating his future, or the many hours he spent in prayer and reflection away in some lonely spot up on the hills. The story of Martha and Mary reminds us that, just as Jesus needed such moments, so we also need to make space in our lives to ponder the things that matter most.

Reading: Luke 10:38-42

As they continued on their way, he entered a certain village, where a woman called Martha welcomed him into her home. She had a sister called Mary, who sat at the Lord's feet, listening to his words. Martha, however, was preoccupied with her many tasks;

21

so she came to him and asked, 'Lord, doesn't it matter to you that my sister has left me to do all the work by myself? Tell her then to lend a hand.' But the Lord answered her, 'Martha, Martha, you are fretting and distracted by many things; only one thing is really important. Mary has chosen that more important thing, and it will not be taken away from her.'

Meditation

I felt sorry for Martha, I really did –
    she was doing her best after all.
Someone had to see to the hospitality,
    make sure the dinner was all right,
    wash up after us,
    and to be honest I felt I wasn't pulling my weight.
I could see she was getting harassed,
    despite the smile she kept on her face.
She didn't say anything, but she didn't need to,
    I could tell by the way she looked that she was angry –
    and with good reason.
It was selfish of me,
    unforgivable,
    but I couldn't help myself.
He was so fascinating,
    so easy to listen to,
    so genuine.
It was as though every word he spoke was for me,
    answering the questions I'd never dared to ask,
    meeting the needs I never even knew existed,
    giving me the sense of purpose I had so longed to find.
How could I get up to wash dishes,
    interrupt him to offer another drink?
It would have been sacrilege.
I knew I might never have another chance like that again,
    and so, shame on me, I sat back and let Martha get on with it.

I wasn't surprised when she finally complained,
  but I was by the answer Jesus gave her.
I expected him to back her up and give me a ticking off –
  after all, fair's fair –
  but instead he praised *me*
  and rebuked *her!*
He spoke gently of course,
  almost tenderly,
  yet it was a rebuke for all that.
I don't know how she felt, but I could have died of embarrassment.
It was my fault, you see,
  I who effectively earned her that reprimand,
  and I expected her to be furious afterwards –
  I know I would have been.
Yet, funnily enough, she wasn't.
She was very quiet for a time,
  very thoughtful,
  and then she told me not to look so guilty,
  for Jesus had been right.
He'd made her face herself for the first time,
  and she realised now she couldn't go on running for ever,
  couldn't go on hoping that being busy would disguise
    the emptiness inside.
She'd been made to stop and ask herself what life was all about,
  and in Jesus she had begun to find the answers.
She's still the efficient hostess, of course –
  always will be.
And me? I'm just as ready to find an excuse for laziness given half
  the chance!
But we've changed, both of us,
  grown closer,
  found inner contentment,
  become more at peace with ourselves
  because through meeting Jesus we've each discovered what
    really counts,
  the one thing we really need.

Prayer

Loving God
 day after day I seem to be so busy,
 life lived at such a hectic pace,
 with never a moment to spare.
Give me strength to do everything that needs to be done,
 but help me also to remember what matters most of all:
 taking time to pause and ponder,
 to take stock of my life and to reflect on your goodness
 so that I might meet with you and hear your voice.
Draw near now, in these few moments of quietness.
Help me to be still,
 in body, mind and spirit,
 and to know your presence,
 through Jesus Christ my Lord.
Amen.

5

It was a wonderful moment
Peter

'When were you converted?' came the question. 'Tell us how you first became a Christian.' The enquiry was sincere, and I responded accordingly, yet there is something about such questions that I find disturbing. In part, I am uneasy with the idea that we can pinpoint the moment of conversion, identifying exactly where and when we came to faith. Many, of course, do experience a definitive moment when they personally commit their lives to Christ, but for many others the process is more gradual, while others still cannot recall a time when they did not believe. The fact is that faith is an ongoing journey; a journey that often begins long before we realise it, and that invariably continues throughout this life and beyond. This brings me to my greatest unease: the possibility that we may equate the moment of our conversion or commitment to Christ with having somehow arrived; with having done all that is needed. The experience of Peter offers a salutary reminder that this is not so. He had responded to the invitation 'Follow me' and had reached a point when he was ready to declare his faith in Jesus as the Christ; yet, if he thought he'd made it as a disciple his illusions were quickly shattered, for the next moment Jesus was labelling him 'Satan'. His commitment was real enough in its way, but it was shallow and incomplete as he had not yet begun to grasp the full implications of discipleship. It was to be a similar story later as, having again affirmed his undying loyalty, he was to deny Jesus three times. Later still, his learning continued as he came to understand that contrary to everything he had always believed, there was no distinction in God's eyes between Jew and Gentile, clean and unclean. Faith was never a finished article; it was always on the production line, being shaped, added to, refined, polished. So it is with us. Never make the mistake of supposing you have made your response and that discipleship can take care of itself. Coming to faith is not a one-off event but an ongoing process; not reaching a destination but stepping out, step by step, along the way.

Reading: Mark 8:27-33

Jesus and his disciples continued on their way to the villages surrounding Caesarea Philippi; and en route he asked his disciples, 'Who do people say that I am?' They answered, 'Some reckon John the Baptist; others, Elijah; and others still, that you're one of the prophets.' 'What about you,' he asked them. 'Who do you say that I am?' Peter answered, 'You are the Christ.' Then he warned them to tell no one about him. And he began to teach them that it was necessary for the Son of Man to suffer many things, to be rejected by the chief priests, the elders and the scribes, to be killed and on the third day to rise again. He made no secret of it. Then Peter, taking him aside, began to reproach him. But he spun round, and seeing the disciples there, he took Peter to task, saying, 'Get behind me, Satan: for you are preoccupied not with the things of God, but the things of man.'

Meditation

It was a wonderful moment –
    I really thought I'd cracked it.
After all the uncertainty,
    all the questions,
    all the confusion,
    I finally believed I understood who he was.
'You're the Messiah!' I told him,
    and he beamed at me with such delight,
    I felt my heart would burst.
No one else had grasped it, you see,
    not properly.

They wondered, of course,
    but like so many others they were still guessing,
    groping in the dark.
He might as well have been Elijah or John for all they realised.
I was different, and Jesus knew it.
'Blessed are you,' he said,
    'for God has revealed this to you and not man.'
What an accolade!
But then it all went wrong –
    just when I felt I'd arrived, the bubble burst,
    and with a vengeance!
I suppose I got carried away,
    never stopped to think –
    typical of me, really.
It's just that it came as such a shock,
    him going on like that about the future,
    everything he had to suffer,
    even talking of death itself –
    all doom and gloom.
I wasn't having any of it.
'Not likely!' I shouted. 'No way!'
I meant no harm,
    I just didn't think such things could happen to the Messiah,
    but you should have seen his face:
    the anger,
    the disappointment.
Satan, he called me!
Can you believe that?
Me, his right-hand man,
    the one who'd just hit the nail on the head,
    the pick of the bunch so I thought –
Satan!
I was hurt at the time,
    cut to the heart if I'm honest,
    but I can see now, all too clearly,
    that he was right and I was wrong.

I still had so much to learn,
   so much to understand,
   and I needed a reprimand, a stern hand,
   if I was to progress any further.
I'd only just begun to glimpse the truth,
   and if I'd have had my way
   it would have meant him denying everything he stood for.
He *was* the Messiah,
   but not in the way that I meant it.
He *had* come to establish his kingdom,
   but in a very different way than we expected.
His was the way of service, sacrifice and self-denial,
   offering his life for the life of the world.
I see that now and I marvel at his love,
   but what I marvel at even more is that
   even when I understood him so little
   he understood me so much!

Prayer

Loving God,
   I thank you for those moments in my life
   that have been milestones in my journey of faith –
   moments when I have been especially conscious of your
     presence,
   when faith has grown,
   when truth has dawned on me in an unmistakable way.
I thank you for such times
   but I ask you to help me always to recognise
   that my journey is not ended but only just begun.
Teach me that however many answers I may have,
   there is always more to see,
   more to learn
   and more to understand.
Through Jesus Christ my Lord.
Amen.

6
'Which am I?' I wondered
Luke

Many of the parables and teachings of Jesus have a disturbing thing in common – they censure the religious people of his day. It is the scribes, Pharisees, priests and Sadducees for whom Jesus typically reserves his sternest denunciations – those convinced of their own righteousness and of their right to judge others. 'Ah yes,' we might say, 'but these were men who were closed to the message of the Gospel. Such words cannot possibly apply to committed Christians and faithful churchgoers today.' To think that is to bury our heads in the sand. Organised religion, Christian or otherwise, is a fertile breeding ground for intolerance, bigotry, self-righteousness and hypocrisy of the worst kind. The more we imagine our lives to be free of such faults, the more likely it is that they have taken hold, as the tale of the Pharisee and tax collector so graphically illustrates. We need always to remember, when reading the parables, that Jesus did not intend them as a pat on the back or reassuring homily, but as a challenge to all who heard them – and that includes you and me today. In this season of reflection and self-examination, is it time we faced up to some awkward truths?

Reading: Luke 18:9-14

He told a further parable to some who were so convinced of their own righteousness that they looked down dismissively on others. 'Two men went up to the temple to pray, the first a Pharisee and the second a tax collector. The Pharisee, standing aloof, prayed like this, "God, I thank you that I am not like other people – corrupt, deceitful, adulterous – or even like this tax collector. I fast twice weekly and tithe all my income." But the tax collector, standing at a distance, could not even bring himself to lift his eyes to heaven, but was beating his breast, saying, "God, be merciful to a miserable sinner like me!" Mark my words, it was this man rather than the other who went home at peace with God; for all who laud their own virtue will be humbled, but those who humble themselves will be exalted.'

Meditation

'Which am I?' I wondered.
'The Pharisee, or the tax collector?'
I'm neither, of course,
    not literally,
    but that wasn't the point was it?
'Which of the two am I most like?' that's what I found myself
    asking,
    and I had a shrewd suspicion I wouldn't much like the answer.
So it proved,
    though perhaps not quite as I feared,
    for, in actual fact, like most of us I'm a bit of both,
    neither all of one or the other.
There are times when I'm the tax collector –
    ashamed of my faithlessness,
    overwhelmed by a sense of failure,
    able only to throw myself on God's goodness
    knowing I have no claim on his love
    nor any reason to expect mercy.
And, at those times, just as Jesus said, I find a sense of peace,
    a feeling of being right with God –
    my sins forgiven,
    the past absolved,
    mistakes over and done with.

Only it never lasts,
    for there's always that other self refusing to be silenced,
    the Pharisee within me straining to break free –
    prim, proper, self-righteous,
    head shaking in disapproval,
    finger pointing in accusation,
    so certain I am right and others wrong.
Can they both be me,
    each part of the same person?
I'm afraid they are, much though it hurts to admit it.
But at least it *does* hurt, that's something;
    for so long as I can still recognise my need,
    still see myself as I really am
    and still feel a sense of shame,
    then it's not all lost –
    there's hope for me even yet.
So I'm here, Lord,
    the two of me together,
    tax collector and Pharisee,
    and my prayer is simply this:
    'God, be merciful to me, a sinner!'

Prayer

Lord Jesus Christ,
    I don't mean to be self-righteous
    but I can be sometimes,
    more often than I may realise.
I claim to be accepting of others,
    but when they do not conform to my expectations
    I make little attempt to conceal my feelings.
I claim to recognise my faults,
    but if anyone points them out to me, I am quick to take offence.
I see the speck in my neighbour's eye
    but time and again overlook the log in my own.

31

Forgive me my innate tendency to assume that I am right
    and others are wrong.
Help me, instead, to understand that, whoever I am,
    I depend finally on your grace,
    and so, recognising the strengths and weaknesses of all,
    may I live in true humility,
    to the glory of your name.
Amen.

7
What a day it was
Simon the Zealot

Palm Sunday is something of an enigma in the Christian calendar. It speaks of joy and celebration, and of worshipping Jesus as the King of kings, and yet of course it leads us into the events of Holy Week, the experience of sorrow and suffering, and finally death on a cross. We cannot think of one without the other, and any talk of the majesty of Jesus must be understood in the light of all that followed. The one we serve came to serve. The Lord of life endured the darkness of death. The way to the throne involved the costly path of sacrifice. It is easy enough to sing Christ's praises and acknowledge him as Lord; it is a different matter to take up our cross and follow him. Yet that is the homage he asks of us, and the challenge this day brings. As we offer today our glad hosannas, let us ask ourselves if we are ready also to offer ourselves in his service.

Reading: Luke 19:36-42

As he rode, people carpeted the road with their cloaks. Then, as he started the descent from the Mount of Olives, the whole multitude of the disciples began loudly and joyfully to praise God for the mighty deeds they had seen, saying, 'Blessed is the king who comes in the name of the Lord! Peace in heaven! Glory in the highest heaven!' Some Pharisees in the crowd said to him, 'Teacher, reprimand your disciples and tell them to stop.' He answered, 'I tell you this, if they were to keep silent, the very stones would shout out.' As he caught sight of the city, he wept over it, saying, 'If only you recognised this day the things that make for peace! Instead, though, they are hidden from your eyes!'

Meditation

What a day it was,
    a day I shall never forget –
    the voices raised in jubilation,
    the arms outstretched in welcome,
    the crowds lining the streets,
    waving their palm branches,
    hurling down their cloaks,
    welcoming their king:
    the Son of David,
    the one who came in the name of the Lord.
They believed that, at long last, the waiting was over,
    the Messiah finally come to set them free.
We believed it too, come to that.
After all his talk of suffering and death,
    we dared to hope he'd got it wrong,
    and for a moment, as I watched him,
    I wondered if he felt the same –
    the way he responded to the cheers,
    laughter playing on his lips,
    a smile on his face,
    a twinkle in his eyes.
He was enjoying himself, I'm sure of that,
    determined to savour the moment.
But then I noticed it
    as we drew near to Jerusalem:
    a tear in the corner of his eye –
    so unexpected.
Not a tear of joy but of sorrow,
    trickling slowly down his face,
    silent testimony to his pain.
He wasn't fooled by the welcome,
    not like the rest of us.
He knew what they wanted,
    how they would change,

but still he continued, resolute to the end –
    that's the extraordinary thing.
It was a day to remember,
    a day on which they welcomed their king.
But none imagined, least of all I,
      that the crown would be made of thorns,
      and the throne reached via a cross.

Prayer

Lord Jesus Christ,
    I remember how you entered Jerusalem
    to shouts of joy and celebration,
    but I remember too how quickly that welcome evaporated,
    how soon the mood of the crowd changed.
I like to think I'm different,
    but deep down I know I'm not –
    my faith just as superficial,
    my commitment just as short-lived,
    my love just as self-centred as theirs.
Help me truly to make you the Lord of my life,
    and to go on serving you,
    come what may,
    now and always,
    to the glory of your name.
Amen.

8
He couldn't mean me, surely?
Philip

How must the Apostles have felt when Jesus turned to them in the upper room with that chilling pronouncement, 'One of you will betray me'? Their response, in the original Greek, literally means 'Not I', but this can be taken in a variety of ways, from an instantaneous denial to a querulous question. Were they certain that Jesus could not mean them, or did his words touch a nerve, exposing the limitations of their commitment? Of Peter, we need ask no further – he was confident that he would never fail, although he would soon learn otherwise. Similarly, if Judas joined in the protestations his words were nothing more than empty deceit, for he was well aware what he had planned for that night. What, though, of the others? We cannot be sure, but I suspect there was genuine uncertainty in their answer. Certainly, they wanted to stay true, but they probably also experienced a moment of self-doubt as they met Jesus' gaze; self-doubt that was to prove well founded as each of them scattered at his arrest, leaving him to face his hour of need alone. Would we have been any different? I don't think I would. Yet here we see the enormity of Christ's love, for he willingly went to his death while fully recognising the weakness of his followers and the feebleness of their faith. We deserve so little, yet he gave so much!

Reading: Mark 14:17-25
When evening fell, he came with the twelve. As they reclined, eating, Jesus said, 'Truly I tell you, one of you will betray me; one eating with me now.' They became agitated, blurting out, one after another, 'You don't mean me, surely?' He said to them, 'It is one of

the twelve, one who is dipping bread into the bowl with me. For the Son of Man goes as it has been written concerning him, but woe to the one who the Son of Man is betrayed by! It would have been better for him not to have been born.' During supper, he took bread, and having given thanks he broke it and gave it to them, saying, 'Take this; it is my body.' Then he took a cup, and, giving thanks to God, he handed it to them; and they all drank from it. Then he said, 'This is my blood, the blood of the covenant, shed for many. I tell you the truth, I will not drink of the fruit of the vine again until that day when I drink it new with you in the kingdom of God.'

Meditation

He couldn't mean me, surely? – that's what I kept telling myself –
   one of the others perhaps, but not me.
I would stay true, if nobody else did,
      dependable to the last,
      someone he could stake his life on if he needed to.
Yet could he?
Deep down, despite my protestations, I wondered,
      for to tell the truth I was scared out of my wits,
      dreading what the future might hold for us.
It was suddenly all too real,
      the prospect of suffering and death,
      those warnings Jesus had given
      no longer simply words we could push aside,
      but fact staring us in the face.
His enemies were gathering for the kill,
      greedily waiting their moment,
      and it was only a matter of time
      before they came for the rest of us.
We'd kept on smiling until then,
      putting a brave face on things as best we could,
      if not for his sake then our own.

But suddenly there could be no running away any longer,
    for in that stark sentence he spelt out the awful truth:
'One of you will betray me.'
We protested, of course, vehement in our denials,
    yet one by one we looked away, unable to meet his gaze.
It *wasn't* me, I'm glad to say,
    but of course you'll know that by now, won't you?
It was Judas who finally couldn't take it.
Judas, whose name will go down in history
    as the one who betrayed Jesus.
Yet somehow that doesn't help, for the truth is this,
    when the moment came we were all found wanting,
    all more concerned for our own safety than his.
Maybe we didn't betray him,
    but don't think we're feeling smug about it,
    still less like twisting the knife in Judas,
    for that moment, there in the upper room,
    made us all take a long hard look at ourselves,
    and we didn't much like what we saw.

Prayer

Merciful God,
    I don't find it easy to be honest with myself,
    for there are some things I prefer to keep hidden
    rather than face the disturbing truth.
Occasionally I catch a glimpse of my darker side
    but I push it away,
    attempting to deny its existence even to myself,
    but the knowledge of my weakness is always there,
    lurking in the shadows.
Help me, then, to open my heart before you
    and to acknowledge my faults,
    in the knowledge that your nature is always to have mercy.

Cleanse,
   redeem,
   renew,
   restore,
   and, by your grace,
   help me to come to terms with the person I am
   so that one day I might become the person you would have me
      be,
   through Jesus Christ my Lord.
Amen.

9

It was heartbreaking to see him
One of the crowd on the way to Golgotha

Imagine how it must have felt to be a follower of Jesus, watching him stagger under the weight of the cross towards the place called Golgotha. You have watched thus far in horror, but now you close your eyes, unable to look any more at the scenes unfolding before you; yet you cannot block out the sounds of what is happening, sounds that are equally if not more dreadful. The ringing of the hammer as it drives the nails mercilessly through the flesh of Jesus. The involuntary gasps of agony as the cross is lifted up and those skewered hands and feet begin to tear under his weight. The raucous jeers of the crowd as they gather round to gloat, their jeers mingled with the sobs of women nearby, their hearts close to breaking. Surely it will be over soon. Nothing can be worse than this! Only then it comes, the most terrible, haunting sound of all; a cry of such torment, such desolation, that your blood runs cold – 'My God, my God, why have you forsaken me?' Suddenly you realise, for the first time, the extent of this man's love; and the depth and awesomeness of his commitment and the immensity of his sacrifice.

Reading: Luke 23:26-31

As they led him away, they seized a man, Simon of Cyrene, who was coming from the country, and they laid the cross on him, and made him carry it behind Jesus. A great number of the people followed him, and among them were women who were beating their breasts and wailing for him. But Jesus turned to them and said, 'Daughters of Jerusalem, do not weep for me, but weep for yourselves and for your children. For the days are surely coming when they will say, 'Blessed are the barren, and the wombs that never bore, and the breasts that never nursed.' Then they will begin to say to the mountains, 'Fall on us'; and to the hills, 'Cover us.' For if they do this when the wood is green, what will happen when it is dry?' (NRSV)

Meditation

It was heartbreaking to see him,
   to watch the man we'd come to love collapsing in agony,
   to witness our dreams founder with him,
   lying broken in the dust.
Suddenly our world was in pieces,
   for it was impossible not to look back
   and remember his words in happier days,
   words that had seemed so full of promise.
'Come to me,' he had said, 'all you that are weary
   and are carrying heavy burdens,
   and I will give you rest.
   'Take my yoke upon you, and learn from me;
   for I am gentle and humble in heart,
   and you will find rest for your souls.
   'For my yoke is easy,
   and my burden is light.'
What could we make of that now
   as he staggered under the weight of that cross,
   crushed by the burden,
   scarcely able to stand,
   finally unable to carry it any longer?
It challenged everything,
   all we had seen and heard,
   all we'd come to believe,
   for how could it be –

the man who'd healed the sick broken beyond recognition,
the one who'd forgiven sins convicted as a common criminal,
the Messiah, who'd promised life, facing the darkness of
    death?
We stood there, horrified,
    unable to make sense of what was happening.
'Why doesn't he do something?' we asked.
'He has the power, so why not use it?'
Surely now, of all times, called for one of his signs and wonders,
    another of those miracles that had captivated the multitudes
        throughout his ministry.
What was he waiting for?
Why the delay?
We just couldn't work it out.
Only then he turned and looked at us,
    a slow, sad smile touching his face,
    and I could see the sorrow he felt was not for him but for us –
    the pain *we* had yet to bear,
    the sorrow we had still to endure as part of this bleeding
        broken world;
    a world he had come to heal through his dying.
It was *still* heartbreaking to watch, despite that knowledge,
    more awful than I can ever tell you,
    but it was no longer a mystery, not to me anyway.
He could have walked away as I'd hoped he might do,
    sparing himself the agony and degradation,
    but he didn't –
    he took the way of the cross,
    bearing our burdens,
    carrying our punishment,
    enduring our darkness,
    dying our death –
    and I understood that he'd produced a miracle after all –
    the greatest sign and wonder we could ever ask for!

Prayer

Sovereign God,
  though I cannot always make sense of your purposes
  teach me that you are still at work.
Though the way may be hidden
  and the path appear dark,
  teach me that you are sometimes most near when you seem
    most distant
Help me to recognise that you are a God who turns sorrow into
  laughter,
  weakness into strength,
  darkness into light
  and death into life;
  who is able to take what seems irredeemably bad and use it for
    good.
Teach me, then, never to despair of any moment,
  however bleak it may seem,
  for you have shown me that there is nothing
  in heaven or earth
  beyond your renewing power.
To you be praise and glory,
  now and always.
Amen.

10

He was in agony
One of the soldiers who crucified Jesus

How would you have acted had you been hanging on the cross in place of Jesus, listening to the sneers and shouts of your enemies as they watch you writhing there in agony? Would you have called curses down upon them from heaven? I think I might have done. Would you have cried out in anger, 'Why me? What have I done to deserve this?' Again, yes, I think I might. Alternatively, would you have been so preoccupied with your pain and misery that you had thoughts for no one but yourself? On reflection, that's probably how I'd have felt. I'm sure I wouldn't have said: 'Father, forgive them, for they do not know what they are doing.' It's amazing – in the most appalling of suffering, to think not simply of others but of those who have brought it upon you. In the throes of death, to ask God to forgive your killers – how many of us could do that? Here is the reason we are here today. Here is the man we come to honour, and the God we meet through him. The God who gives and goes on giving; who loves and goes on loving; who suffered and goes on suffering until that day when each and every one of us has responded to his grace and been gathered into his kingdom. Pause now, reflect, and worship him.

Reading: Luke 23:33-36

When they reached the place called 'The Skull', they crucified him with the criminals, one on his right and one on his left. Then Jesus said, 'Father, forgive them, for they do not understand what they are doing.' Then, dividing up his clothes, they cast lots for them. The people stood by, watching, but the leaders taunted him, saying,

'He saved others. If he is the Christ, the chosen one of God, let him save himself!' The soldiers also mocked him, coming up and offering him wine-vinegar, with the words, 'If you are the King of the Jews, save yourself!'

Meditation

He was in agony –
    believe me, I know.
I've seen it often enough, crucifixion –
    all in a day's work for me,
    and I've heard a few howl for mercy over the years.
There's few things to touch it, so they tell me, for sheer pain –
    slow, lingering, dreadful.
But he was different, that was the curious thing.
I could see he was suffering all right;
    it was there in his eyes,
    in the gritted teeth,
    in the writhing body,
    in the sweat pouring from him,
    and most of all in that last awful groan.
But he never complained,
    never screamed,
    never swore.
Funny that.
To be honest, I've never seen anyone quite like him –
    that look he had, even in death,
    as though *we* were the ones suffering,
    as though *we* were the criminals deserving punishment,
    as though *he* felt sorry for *us*.
Ridiculous, of course,
    but you know, I could swear as he drew his last breath
    there was a smile on his face,
    almost like he felt he'd achieved something.
An odd business,
    very odd.